A DOCUMENTARY HISTORY OF THE HOLOCAUST™

THE WARSAW GHETTO AND UPRISING

JERI FREEDMAN

ROSEN PUBLISHING®
New York

Published in 2015 by The Rosen Publishing Group, Inc.
29 East 21st Street, New York, NY 10010

First Edition

Library of Congress Cataloging-in-Publication Data

Freedman, Jeri, author.
The Warsaw ghetto and uprising/Jeri Freedman.
p. cm.—(A documentary history of the Holocaust)
Includes bibliographical references and index.
ISBN 978-1-4777-7605-6 (library bound)
1. Warsaw (Poland)—History—Warsaw Ghetto Uprising, 1943—Juvenile literature. 2. Holocaust, Jewish (1939-1945)—Poland—Warsaw—Juvenile literature. 3. World War, 1939-1945—Jewish resistance—Poland—Warsaw—Juvenile literature. 4. World War, 1939-1945—Jews—Poland—Warsaw—Jews—Juvenile literature. 5. Warsaw (Poland)—Ethnic relations—Juvenile literature. I. Title.
D765.2.W3F69 2015
940.53'1853841--dc23

2013039270

Manufactured in the United States of America

CONTENTS

INTRODUCTION

After the German occupation of Warsaw, many displaced Jews relied on Jewish social organizations' soup lines for food, such as this one, and street markets to purchase necessary items or sell personal possessions to raise money.

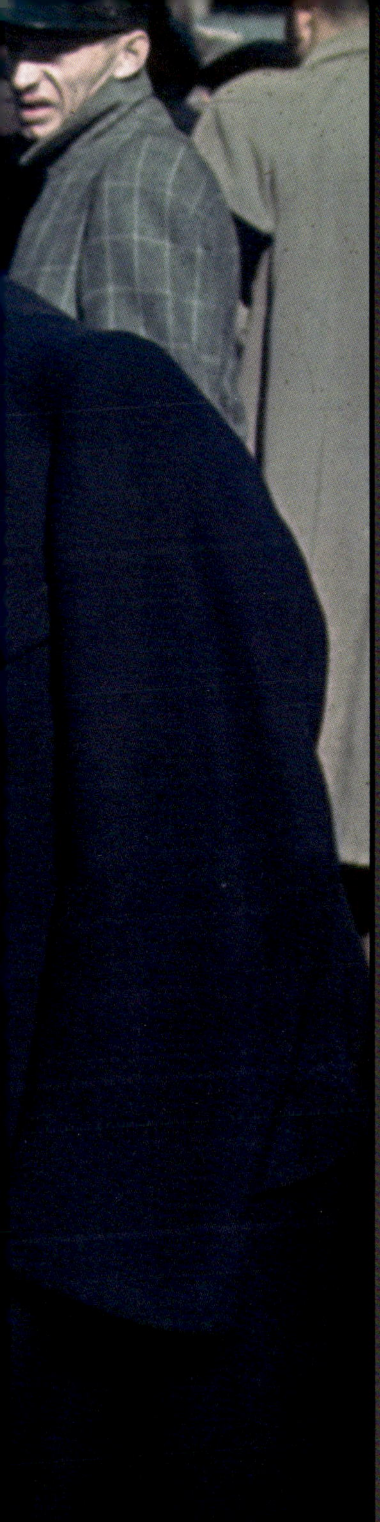

When the Nazis rose to power in Germany during the 1930s, they developed a plan to create a new world order. In the Nazi view of the world, pure Aryan Germans would rule the world. As a first step in this transformation, inferior people, deemed to be corrupting influences, would be eliminated. Although the Nazis targeted a number of groups, including Gypsies, communists, and homosexuals, their chief target was Jews.

The formation and destruction of the Warsaw Ghetto by the Nazis is one of the most iconic events of the period. The German invasion of Poland in 1939 gave the Nazi regime the opportunity to implement its master plan to eliminate the Jews of Europe in a large-scale extermination program. The plan encompassed confining the Jews in a restricted area to make their survival difficult, followed by mass transportation of surviving Jews to concentration camps, where they were killed.

In the face of hardship in the ghetto, the Jews did not give up, however. They formed social organizations to help those who suffered there. They also formed underground resistance organizations. To the surprise of their Nazi oppressors, they did not go quietly to their deaths but engaged in armed resistance that lasted twenty-eight days. The causes of the formation of the ghetto, daily life in the ghetto, the events that led to the Warsaw Ghetto uprising, and the aftermath of the uprising are covered in the material included here.

The Warsaw Ghetto no longer exists, but its history provides insight into many aspects of the Nazis' attempts to eliminate the Jewish population of Europe and the suffering of the Jews. It also illustrates the extraordinary efforts of people to survive under horrendous circumstances and to help each other. Above all, the events in the Warsaw Ghetto demonstrate how people can respond with tremendous courage in the face of impossible odds.

CHAPTER 1

THE WAR AGAINST THE JEWS

The rise of the National Socialist German Workers' (Nazi) Party in Germany was largely the result of events following the end of World War I (1914–1918). When Germany lost World War I, the Allied powers, which won the war—primarily England, France, Russia, and the United States—imposed harsh measures on the defeated German state. Among these were forcing Germany to accept responsibility for causing the war and imposing huge monetary payments for damages resulting from the war. The measures enacted by the Allies put immense strain on the German economy. They also offended German pride. After the war, the ruler of Germany, Kaiser Wilhelm, was forced to abdicate, and democracy was established. However, the democratic government was weak and seen by many Germans as a pawn of the Allied powers.

With the economy in ruins and the populace angry, the stage was set for the rise of populist *völkisch* political movements, which celebrated traditional Germanic folk culture. These movements glorified Germany's cultural and military past and blamed the loss of the war and the decline of Germany on "corrupting influences" that had contaminated

This 1933 photograph shows a group promoting traditional German culture in Wittenberg Square in Berlin, appealing to Germany's pride in its past.

Germany. Chief among the groups blamed by these movements were the Jews, because they were seen as promoting decadent liberal views and financing the Allies. Anti-Semitism, or prejudice against Jews, became rampant.

Ultimately, the Nazi Party, under the leadership of Adolf Hitler, emerged as the most successful *völkisch* political party. The Nazi rhetoric appealed to downtrodden Germans' pride. The party told them that Germany's losing World War I and Germany's subsequent problems weren't the fault of Germans. Instead it was the Jews who were to blame because they had promoted liberal ideas that weakened traditional German values, and they had worked from inside Germany to sabotage the war effort. The Nazis also promoted the myth that the Jews were secretly controlling the world economy, and they were responsible for the miserable state of Germany's economy.

The Nazis promoted the idea that Germans were the direct descendants of an ancient "master race," dubbed "Aryans," who had developed superior skills and come to dominate the ancient world. Other peoples, such as Jews and all dark-skinned people, were declared to be descendants of inferior "races." Thus, the Germans were destined to rule the world, and it was only the corruption and contamination of inferior people that kept them from achieving that goal.

THE NEW WORLD ORDER

The Nazis proposed an agenda that would establish a new world order and restore Germany to its rightful place as the most powerful nation in the world. A cornerstone of this policy was racial purity. Only by eliminating people who corrupted pure German blood could Germans again become pure Aryans. Aryans, being superior to other people, would naturally rule over others.

The Nazi party political platform included the following:

- To unify all Germanic people. Provinces of other countries that contained large ethnically German populations (for example, parts of France and Poland) would be taken over and become part of Germany.
- The peace treaties of Versailles and Saint-Germain, which imposed unpopular measures on

Germany and forbade them from forming a military, would be revoked.

- Germany had the right to take land and form colonies to feed the German people and settle the surplus population.
- Only people of pure ethnic German descent would be considered citizens of Germany and have the right to vote and hold political office.
- The state would have the right to deport noncitizens (people who weren't pure Germans) if there weren't enough resources to go around.
- There would be a redistribution of wealth so that all Germans would find themselves better off economically.

In the face of the democratic government's inability to solve the social and economic problems of the German people, the Nazi Party gained increasing support. In 1933, Adolf Hitler became chancellor (head of the government) of Germany. In April 1933, the government passed the Enabling Act, which allowed Adolf Hitler, and thus the Nazi Party, to assume control of the government. The period of Nazi governance is referred to as the Third Reich. (The First Reich being the monarchy, and the Second Reich being the period of democratic governance.) Once they had control, the Nazis set about achieving their objectives. They began systematically implementing actions that would rid Germany of corrupting influences, especially Jews, and began to prepare for the military invasion of Europe.

LEGISLATING AGAINST THE JEWS

The Nazi Party enacted a series of laws to provide the legal foundation that allowed them to forcibly take the life, liberty,

THE ANTI-JEWISH LAWS AND SCHOOLCHILDREN

Shortly after the Nazis assumed power, they began to engage in activities that affected Jewish schoolchildren. The Germans saw education as a means to indoctrinate young people and control the population. Jewish teachers and professors were fired from schools and universities. The number of Jewish schoolchildren allowed to attend schools was reduced, supposedly to lessen overcrowding and allow better resources for German students. Less than 1 percent of the population of universities was allowed to be Jewish because this was the percentage of Jews in the population of Germany.

According to the London Jewish Cultural Centre, "Initially, many teachers ignored the political changes. However, very soon, those German teachers who supported the Nazis or had been converted to Nazism began to develop new daily rituals and routines. Many of the 32 percent of teachers who became Nazi Party members would wear their uniform to school."

Textbooks were rewritten to support Nazi propaganda on subjects such as racial purity, and teachers often humiliated Jewish children. For instance, they might make Jewish children stand at the front of the class while they pointed out their "inferior" physical characteristics as part of a biology lesson. German students were a threat as well. Often members of the Hitler Youth would attack male Jewish students on their way to and from school. In 1938, Jewish children were banned from German schools completely.

and property of Jews. These laws paved the way for activities such as the formation of the Warsaw Ghetto. Among these laws were:

In this photograph taken around 1935, German chancellor Adolf Hitler *(in front)* and German minister of war Werner von Blomberg are greeted by crowds and a military band.

- Jews living in Germany were considered to be aliens (noncitizens) and could be expelled; those from abroad were forbidden to enter the country.
- Jews could vote only within their Jewish communities, not in German elections.
- Jews could not study in German educational institutions. Jewish teachers could not teach German children, and German teachers could not teach Jewish children.

- Jews were forced to take Jewish first and last names; those with German names had to change them.
- Jewish reporters could write only for Jewish publications.
- Jewish professionals such as doctors could treat only Jewish people.
- Jewish farmers had to sell their land to German farmers, and Jewish businesses had to be marked with the Star of David (the six-pointed star).
- Jews could not join German organizations.
- Civil servants had to provide proof they were Aryan.

A person was considered to be Jewish if he or she had one Jewish parent or grandparent.

Jews were forced to wear the Star of David on their clothing. This allowed the authorities to instantly identify them. It also made them easy targets for anti-Semitism and violence.

CHAPTER 2

THE JEWS OF WARSAW AND THE "FINAL SOLUTION"

The Nazi plan for world domination began with the invasion of Poland. The Nazis planned to eliminate the Jews of Europe. Poland provided them with the ideal situation in which to perfect the process of extermination.

THE JEWS OF WARSAW

Jews had lived in Warsaw since the 1400s. Originally, they lived in specific areas of the city belonging to the princes of Mazovia, a territory in east-central Poland. Royalty at that time relied on Jews for financing because Christians were forbidden from engaging in moneylending. Jews were primarily merchants, moneylenders, and doctors because they were forbidden by law to own land or practice many trades. The Jews lived in the Old City Market Place, one of the busiest areas of the town near the market square and near the town flour mills next to the town walls. The Jews had their own bathhouse, slaughterhouse, cemetery, and school.

At the end of the fifteenth century, pressure from the Christian religious establishment and the businessmen of Warsaw, who suffered from competition from Jews in trade, forced the monarchy to expel the Jews from Warsaw. The Jews never strayed far from the city, however,

Jewish merchants played an important role in the commerce of Warsaw. They supplied the markets with a wide range of goods both manufactured and imported. This photograph was taken in the Jewish community in Warsaw prior to 1914.

and often entered the city to sell goods or provide services to the royal court when it was in residence. By the mid-eighteenth century, the ban was undermined by the implementation of a system that required Jews in Warsaw to pay a fee to stay there. In response to pressure from merchant and crafts guilds, who again faced competition from the Jews, the government forbade the Jews from living on the left bank of the Vistula River, which runs through the center of Warsaw. They took up residence in an area on the right bank of the river, called Praga. In 1775, a government resolution made it legal for Jews to live in Praga, and it became a major Jewish settlement. Throughout the late eighteenth century, pogroms (organized attacks) against the Jews of the Warsaw area repeatedly took place. Their houses and business were ransacked, and they were often beaten. City officials alternated between banning Jews from the city and allowing certain Jews, primarily tradespeople and shopkeepers, to stay there to provide needed services. By the end of the eighteenth century, Jews were 8 percent of the population of Warsaw. Although their major settlement was Praga, they also lived in certain sections of the left bank area of Warsaw, such as the Old City. It became legal for Jews to live there as long as they paid a tax to do so.

Because Warsaw was the capital city and offered attractive economic opportunities, the Jewish community began to grow. From 8 percent of the population in the mid-1700s, the number of Jews in the city rose to almost 45 percent of the population by 1917. In 1809, the king of Poland, Frederick Augustus, issued an edict forbidding the Jews to live in certain areas where they had traditionally dwelled, such as the Old City and marketplace area, because the overcrowding in these areas was seen as dangerous. A new Jewish district formed in the area around Królewska and Marszalkowska Streets. In 1821, another edict forbade the Jews from living

This pre-1939 photograph from the Jewish Historical Institute in Warsaw shows the Judaic Science Institute on the left and the Great Synagogue on the right. Only the institute survived World War II.

in some of the streets in that area. The effect concentrated the large Jewish population in an even smaller area. In 1832, the city was divided into twelve districts. The Jews lived primarily in District IV, in the upper-center part of the city. This area was officially designated the Jewish district. Smaller Jewish enclaves existed on the northwest edge of the city and in the central area on the east-central side of the river.

By 1939, Warsaw had the second-largest population of Jews of any city. (New York had the largest.) Some of the Jews living

Nalewki Street, part of the Nalewki-Muranów district of Warsaw, is seen here around 1914. This main street had trolley cars running on it since about 1881, but when the Germans occupied the city in 1939, the trolley service was suspended here.

in Warsaw were affluent and they often were assimilated (behaved in the same manner as the rest of the population). However, many who lived in the northern sector of the city were poor. Jews represented about 29 percent of the population of the city at this time. They were concentrated primarily in an area near the center of the city on the northwest side of the river, referred to as the Nalewki-Muranów district. This area was old and overcrowded, which led to it being referred to as a "ghetto," a term that refers to a place where a minority group is forced to live because of social or financial pressure. Inhabitants lived in

A CHILD IN GERMAN-OCCUPIED WARSAW

On the U.S. Holocaust Memorial Museum "Personal Histories" Web site, Benjamin "Ben" Meed describes his experiences as a child shortly after the German invasion of Warsaw. His experience illustrates the anti-Semitism of the period. From the time that the Germans occupied Warsaw, Ben and others living in the city were short of food and hungry. He was desperate to find any kind of food. Finally, he heard that a few trucks with bread to give out had arrived in the area near the Jewish quarter where he lived. He and his brother and sister ran to the trucks.

> **We saw the trucks, looking only at the big trucks with bread, our eyes shined up that we're going to get a piece of bread. There were so many people waiting in the line [that] the bread was not given out. There were two Germans on the trucks throwing out the breads, and there I saw there were in that time cameras filming this whole thing, how they throwing bread to the population. And I was also waiting to grab a loaf of bread, but somehow I was recognized by one of my neighbors. He says, "What *are* you doing here? This is bread for the *Poles*." I says, "So I'm here." He says, "You a *Jew*." That was the first day when I was probably shocked and will never forget. [Italics added for emphasis.]**

[Source: "Benjamin Meed—Oral History. Transcript." Retrieved September 20, 2013 (http://www.ushmm.org/wlc/en/media_oi.php?ModuleId=10007256&MediaId=1095).]

"THE JEWISH QUESTION IN OCCUPIED TERRITORY"

The man responsible for dealing with "the Jewish problem" was Reinhard Heydrich, chief of the Reich's security office. On September 21,1939, he distributed a letter to the chiefs of the security police in which he defined the policies and procedures for handling the Jewish population of occupied territories such as Poland. The subject was "The Jewish Question in Occupied Territory." The letter stated that the final aim—the elimination of the Jews—was to be kept secret. The first prerequisite for the final aim was the concentration of Jews from the countryside into larger cities. Jews were to be concentrated in as few central areas as possible, near railroads (which would allow convenient deportation of Jews). The land belonging to Jews engaged in agriculture was to be handed over to German or Polish farmers. The chiefs of security police were told to set dates to move the Jews in their regions to the city ghettos, including compiling a list of those working in essential industries or provisioning troops.

Heydrich's letter declared that Judenräte, Jewish councils, were to be set up, composed of up to twenty-four Jewish male representatives of the community. These councils would interact with the German authorities and be responsible for carrying out the directives of the Nazis. One of their first assignments was to perform a census of the Jews in their community. The Judenräte were seen as the key to keeping tabs on and controlling the Jewish population of occupied areas.

crowded tenements (rundown apartment buildings) located on streets lined with small shops and stalls selling produce, kosher meat, and handmade and secondhand goods. The streets were filled with people buying, selling, and transacting business.

THE INVASION OF POLAND

Germany invaded Poland on September 1, 1939. It took only weeks for the German army to defeat the Polish army. The Germans declared that the northern territories of Poland that had once been part of Germany were once again part of Germany. These territories included West Prussia, Poznan, Upper Silesia, and what had been the Free City of Danzig. The balance of Poland, including Warsaw, was placed under the General Government. The head of this General Government was Hans Frank, a lawyer for the Nazi Party. He was given the title governor general. Upon seizing control, the Germans

This map shows troop movements during the invasion of Poland in 1939. The German forces attacked from the west while the Soviet Union invaded from the east.

German field marshal Hermann Göring is pictured here in a studio portrait around 1939. The founder of the Gestapo (the German secret police), Göring played a key role in implementing the "Final Solution" to what the Nazis called "the Jewish problem."

issued an edict requiring Jews to wear a yellow Jewish star on their clothing so they could easily be identified. The General Government declared that Jews were to be organized into battalions and forced to perform labor for the benefit of the German war effort.

LABORATORY FOR ELIMINATION

The Nazis used Poland as a test site to perfect procedures to control and ultimately eliminate Jews. The formation of ghettos was conceived by Hermann Göring, a leader in the Nazi Party, in 1938 as a way of concentrating Jews in one local area where they could easily be impressed into forced labor. This concept became one of the cornerstones of the Nazi approach to the Jewish problem. Placing Jews in ghettos also isolated them from the larger population, thus minimizing the chances of Jews receiving outside help. The Jews in the ghettos were organized into battalions and forced to work in quarries and coal mines, in construction, and in factories making armaments and other goods for use by the military. Many of the Jews performing forced labor were eventually transferred to detention camps, where they were made to work while being imprisoned.

CHAPTER 3

DEATH CASKETS

From the beginning, one of the Nazis' major goals was to eliminate Jews. One way to accomplish this objective was to engineer the environment so that the Jews would perish naturally. The formation of ghettos such as the Warsaw Ghetto provided a means to this end.

MADNESS AND DEATH

The Nazi regime had two goals in forming the Polish Jewish ghettos: to bring about the natural death of the Jewish population and subsequently to take their property. Forcing the Jews to do hard forced labor was seen as a method of both helping the war effort and causing the natural death of a large number of Jews. In addition, the Nazi leadership realized that concentrating a large number of Jews in a small area, depriving them of ways of making a living, and preventing them from receiving supplies would result in starvation and disease. Another part of this inhuman plan was for those who did not die to be driven mad through

German soldiers search men in the Warsaw Ghetto. Keeping Jews from obtaining much-needed food and supplies from outside the ghetto was a means of speeding up their elimination.

starvation and misery. Joseph Goebbels, Reich minister of propaganda, called such ghettos "death caskets."

LEADERSHIP IN THE WARSAW GHETTO: ADAM CZERNIAKOW

The chairman of the Judenrat, or Jewish council, in the Warsaw Ghetto was Adam Czerniakow. The Judenrat was formed at the direction of the Nazis. Its role was to inform the Jews in the ghetto of the dictates of the German authorities and to carry out the orders imposed by Nazis for Jews in the ghetto.

Adam Czerniakow was a chemical engineer and past member of the Polish senate. He was an assimilated Jew and had taken no part in the running of the Jewish community in Warsaw. When the Germans invaded Poland, the head of the Jewish community council fled the city, and the mayor of Warsaw asked Czerniakow to take on the role of head of the Jewish community. In 1939, he was ordered by the Germans to establish a Judenrat to run the Jewish community in Warsaw. The Judenrat functioned as the municipal authority responsible for areas such as health, work, food, culture, sanitation, and housing in the ghetto. Czerniakow tried to cooperate with the Nazis to save Jewish lives and keep the Nazis out of the ghetto as much as possible. The resistance movements in the ghetto saw such cooperation differently and accused Czerniakow of collaborating with the Nazis.

In July 1942, when the Nazis began deportations of Jews from the ghetto to the death camps at Treblinka, they demanded that Czerniakow collect Jews for "resettlement to the east." Czerniakow knew the Jews were to be killed, not resettled, and rather than cooperate he committed suicide. According the Yad Vashem Shoah Resource Center in Jerusalem, "Some say that he left a note to his wife explaining his actions: 'They are demanding that I kill the children of my people with my own hands. There is nothing for me to do but to die.'"

LEADERSHIP IN THE WARSAW GHETTO: ADAM CZERNIAKOW (CONTINUED)

Czerniakow left a 1,009-page diary chronicling the events in the Warsaw Ghetto from 1939 until his death, including information on the German invasion, the formation of the ghetto, and the beginning of deportations. Today, the diary forms part of the collection of Yad Vashem.

THE GHETTO IN WARSAW

Arguments constructed by the Nazis to justify the formation of the Warsaw Ghetto included these:

- It was necessary politically to distinguish Poles from Jews.
- Jews were engaged in the black market, and stabilizing the economy required containing them so they couldn't trade in goods.
- The Jews were infected with contagious diseases, such as tuberculosis, and vermin, such as lice, and this represented a threat to the German army and Polish population.

In fact, the Jews were not necessarily different from the rest of the Polish population in terms of their health and activities, but these falsehoods allowed the Nazis to explain to anyone who learned of their actions why they needed to form the ghetto.

Construction of the walls that would enclose the Warsaw Ghetto began on October 12, 1940, the Jewish high holy

This 1941 photograph shows part of the wall enclosing the Warsaw Ghetto. At that time, the walls concentrated a population of approximately four hundred thousand people within the ghetto.

day of Yom Kippur. The Jews of Warsaw, who represented 29 percent of the city's population, were forced to live in an area that consisted of only 2.4 percent of the city's space. Eventually the ghetto's population would rise to nearly 500,000 people. The German authorities published a map showing where Jews could and could not live. In November 1940, the ghetto was sealed off with walls separating it from the rest of the city. The walls were 11.5 feet (3.5 meters) tall and topped by barbed wire. The Jewish community was forced to pay the German construction firm responsible for building the wall. The German authorities called the sealed off area "the Jewish quarter." A German attorney, Heinz Auerswald, was appointed kommisar of the Jewish quarter with authority over the Jews in the enclosed area.

SECURING THE GHETTO

Once the ghetto was walled in, guards were placed at the entrance, strictly controlling traffic into and out of the ghetto. Within the ghetto, an organization of two thousand Jewish police was established. This organization was called the Jüdischer Ordnungsdienst (Jewish Order Service) and was charged with keeping order within the ghetto. Nonetheless, although it was called the Jewish Order Service, the chief and deputy chief of the service were not Jews, but Poles.

Another security force in the ghetto was the Office to Combat Profiteering and Speculation. It was more commonly referred to as "13" because of its address on Leszno Street. Its main division was the Office to Combat Usury and Profiteering in the Jewish Quarter of Warsaw. The members of this organization were Jews who collaborated

This 1942 photograph shows young smugglers climbing over one of the ghetto walls. Smuggling was necessary to avoid starvation, but getting caught could mean imprisonment or death.

(voluntarily cooperated) with the Nazi authorities. The organization reported directly to the German secret police and had its own prosecutor and jail. Its three to four hundred officers were supposed to combat black market activities but often engaged in extorting money from the inhabitants instead. For example, they often discovered suspected smugglers because they were making or selling foodstuffs with ingredients that were unavailable legally in the ghetto, such as meat, sugar, fat, or fish. They would then make that person pay them to avoid being put on trial and jailed.

CHAPTER 4

LIFE IN THE GHETTO

The Warsaw Ghetto was the largest ghetto in any territory conquered by the Nazis. Its area covered approximately 1.3 square miles (3.37 square kilometers), including part of the Wola, Śródmieście, and Stare Miasto (the Old City) districts. Sealed off from the outside world, the inhabitants were dependent on the German authorities for necessities. The Germans enforced severe limitations on goods that they allowed to be brought into the ghetto. The enforced shortage of food, materials, and services made life in the ghetto extremely difficult, but the people of the ghetto met these challenges with resourcefulness.

EARNING A LIVING

According to the Aktion Reinhard Camps and the Holocaust Education and Archive Research Team, an organization of Holocaust researchers, in 1941 Adam Czerniakow, head of the Judenrat in the Warsaw Ghetto, "estimated that there were about 10,000 ghetto inhabitants with capital, 250,000 who could support themselves, and 150,000 who were destitute."

A peddler in the Warsaw Ghetto sells mousetraps. Many inhabitants of the ghetto made items at home or in small workshops to sell to earn money.

There were two sources of income in the ghetto. Beginning in spring 1941, because of the need for goods to support the war effort, various German companies were allowed to set up small factories, called "workshops," in the ghetto. Because Jews were paid very little, they were a cheap source of labor. Jews in the ghetto also showed remarkable resourcefulness in setting up their own manufacturing operations. Such factories were illegal, and materials had to be smuggled in from outside the ghetto. Smuggling took place through buildings connected to both the Jewish and Aryan quarters, and canals that ran under the city. Policemen, guards, and Germans and Poles who traveled to and from the ghetto were also bribed to bring goods in and out. Children were often used in smuggling operations. They were small, fast, and often unnoticed by adults going about their business. According to Adam Czerniakov, food accounted for 80 percent of the goods smuggled into the ghetto.

Items produced in the ghetto workshops and factories—for both internal and external use—included brushes and brooms; aluminum bowls, cutlery, stoves, and pipes; leather goods; soap; clothing; shoes; hats; toys; chemicals; furniture; and miscellaneous household items. Commerce within the ghetto took place primarily in small shops and street stalls. The most commonly sold goods were food of various types, clothing, books, and small craft items. Services such as hairdressing, mending, and photography were also offered.

CULTURE IN THE GHETTO

The transmission of Jewish culture was kept alive by secret organizations such as the Idische Kultur Organizacje (Yiddish Culture Organization), founded by Emmanuel Ringelblum and Menahem Linder. Ringelblum was a

A CHILD IN THE WARSAW GHETTO

Economist Ed Herman was a child in the Warsaw Ghetto. As he recalls in the *Frontline* article "Ed Herman: My Warsaw Ghetto Memories":

> **In October of 1940, the Warsaw ghetto was established; over 400,000 people were packed into an area of 1.3 square miles [3.4 sq km]. The Nazis decreed that all Jews had to live within its boundaries, and for identification purposes had to wear armbands with the Star of David. I saw much suffering around me. The ghetto was very overcrowded. There was a typhoid epidemic. Many buildings, including the one in which I lived with my grandfather, were under quarantine. From our windows I could see the inside of the ghetto wall.**
>
> **During the winter I was very cold; to keep warm I stayed in bed covered by whatever I could find. I was continuously hungry. Because of flour shortages the meager bread rations that we received contained sawdust. I was dreaming of the white Kaiser rolls that I had for breakfast before the war in Katowice. In the ghetto, young starving children were begging for food, dead bodies were just lying in the streets. . . .**

In Warsaw Herman had relatives who lived near the Pawiak prison run by the Gestapo. To visit his relatives, he had to cross the police checkpoint. One day on the way to a visit he was beaten by a policeman "for no reason at all, simply because I was there."

[Source: WGBH Educational Foundation/PBS. "Ed Herman: My Warsaw Ghetto Memories." *Frontline*. May 14, 2013. Retrieved September 20, 2013 (http://www.pbs.org/wgbh/pages/frontline/biographies/never-forget-to-lie/ed-herman-my-warsaw-ghetto-memories/).]

historian who collected papers, notes, and diaries from people in the Warsaw Ghetto. His collection provides much of the information people know about the ghetto today. Linder was a community activist and member of the underground. The organization sponsored literary evenings to promote Yiddish culture. Writers and poets continued to produce works in the ghetto, and a secret library circulated books. Theatrical troupes and a symphony orchestra gave performances as well.

Ringelbaum established a secret archive under the code name Oneg Shabbat (Joy of the Sabbath). He collected documents, notes, diaries, and underground newspapers totaling tens of thousands of pages. This archive provides much of the information relied on today for information on what occurred in the ghetto.

The only newspapers allowed in the ghetto were those publishing material that was approved by the Nazis, containing information such as directives. Thus, the Jews were desperate for information that reflected the truth about German activities and what was really happening outside the ghetto walls. Underground newspapers were published, providing information about the war and German activities.

WELFARE IN THE GHETTO

Rations given by German authorities to the Jews of the Warsaw Ghetto were under two hundred calories per day compared to about eight hundred calories for other Poles. By comparison, approximately two thousand calories per day is considered a healthy intake of calories for an adult, and this is the amount Germans could get with their ration cards. Jews in the ghetto responded to the lack of food by smuggling food

Even in the dire circumstances of the Warsaw Ghetto, the inhabitants kept Jewish culture alive. This 1941 photo shows a boy playing the violin to earn money.

into the ghetto. The problem of how to feed the vast number of destitute people who could not buy food, legal or illegal, was a pressing issue. Soup kitchens were organized to provide a midday meal of six hundred to eight hundred calories. Almost every apartment house also had a "house committee." This committee collected money from all the inhabitants to provide help to those who needed it as well as fix the apartment building itself when necessary. The committee members went from apartment to apartment collecting food and money from those who could afford to contribute and then distributed it to those who were destitute. Despite these efforts, starvation was the leading cause of death in the ghetto, accounting for most of the five thousand deaths per month.

Many groups and neighborhood associations set up soup kitchens where people could obtain a bowl of soup for free or for a small fee. The main ingredients of the soup were vegetables and kasha (ground buckwheat) or barley. Charitable organizations such as Jewish Social Self-Help (Zydowska Samopomoc Spoleczna, or ZSS) supported many of these soup kitchens. By May 1941, people who had registered for help at these kitchens numbered 115,400. The food situation was so dire that the Judenrat took over administration of the soup kitchens in an attempt to provide meals to a greater number of people. By September, the kitchens were giving out 128,000 meals. For many people, it was their only meal of the day.

As might be imagined, there were a large number of orphaned children in the ghetto, and the number grew as time went on. Organizations such as the Central Organization for Orphan Care (CENTOS) set up orphanages to house homeless children. The biggest problem was finding food to feed the children. Despite practical hardships, CENTOS also made efforts to educate the children in its care. The organization also set up daycare rooms in many of the

The enormous death toll in the ghetto left a large number of children orphans. Without parents to provide for them, these children often ended up living in the streets.

tenements in the ghetto, where workers attempted to educate and entertain the children.

HEALTH CARE IN THE GHETTO

Whenever people are forced into overcrowded situations, they quickly pass diseases to one another. Despite the establishment of hospitals and clinics, epidemics of diseases such as typhus and tuberculosis were common, and large numbers of people died. When there was no money to pay for burial, it was common to see unburied corpses in the street. The ghetto was sealed off in November 1940. By August 1941 the monthly death toll was four thousand to five thousand per month, and it remained at that level until the ghetto's destruction. (Today many Jews of eastern European ancestry are more resistant to tuberculosis than members of other ethnic groups because they are the descendants of those who were resistant to the disease in the ghettos created by the Nazis and, therefore, survived.)

Under the direction of the Judenrat, two hospitals and a number of clinics were set up in the ghetto and staffed by the doctors, nurses, and medical aides in the ghetto. However, these hospitals were too overcrowded and understaffed to deal with the huge number of patients. There were also pharmacies in the ghetto, but they were always short of medications, as the German and Polish agencies that were supposed to supply them often failed to do so or supplied inadequate amounts. As a result, medications had to be smuggled into the ghetto.

Because of the dire nature of the health situation, the ZSS organized a private health service. The ZSS's Department of Health engaged in improving hygiene and providing

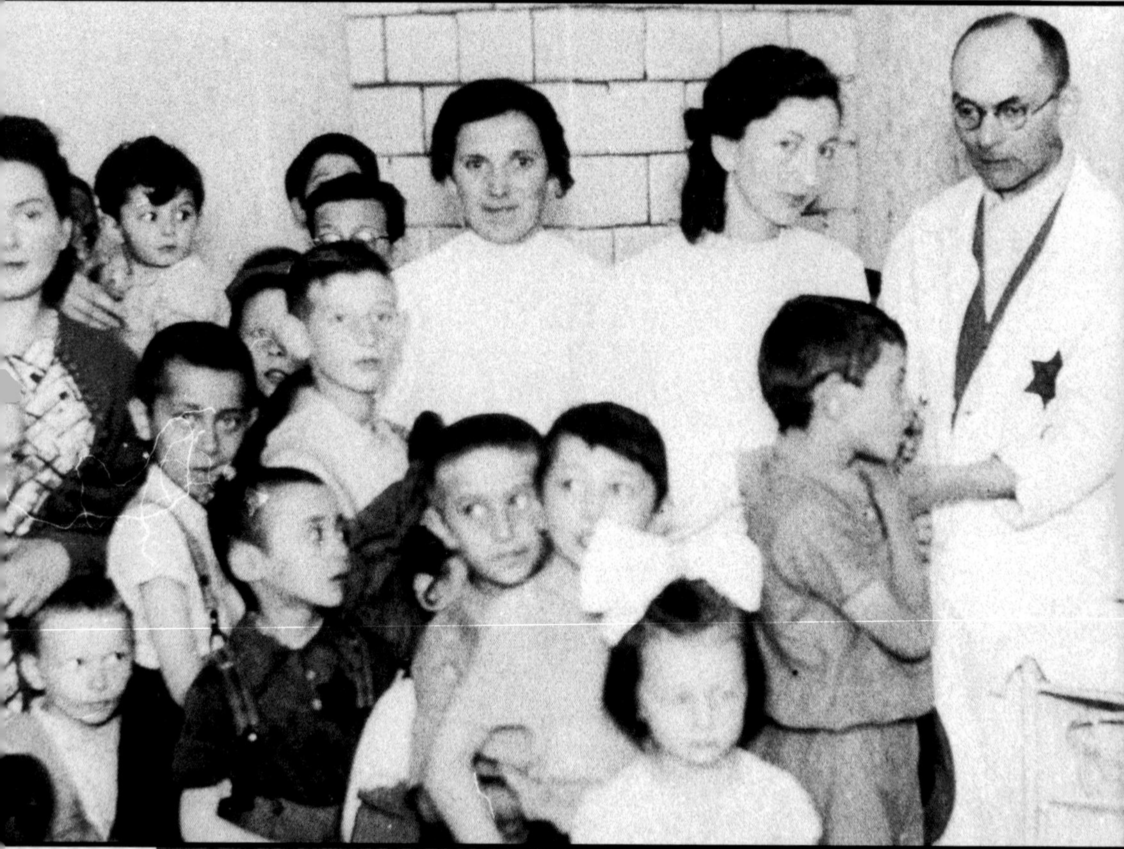

Organizations such as the ZSS sought to provide basic health care for children in the ghetto. Here, children wait for examinations in a Warsaw Ghetto clinic in 1940.

medical care, especially to those who could not afford private medical care. The ZSS also established the Doctors' Emergency Service, which included an ambulance service and doctors who worked at hospitals and clinics. Another charitable organization that provided health care services was the Society for the Protection of the Jewish Population in Poland, which was founded in 1922 to educate Jews about ways to improve their health. In the ghetto, this organization set up tuberculosis, dermatological, and dental clinics, among other activities.

SAVING THE CHILDREN

Amid the brutal events taking place in the Warsaw Ghetto, there were also amazing moments of heroism. At a time when many Poles were ignoring the actions the Nazis were taking against the Jews, a Polish social worker, Irena Sendler, took extraordinary measures that saved the lives of many Jewish children.

When the Germans invaded Poland in 1939, Sendler was a senior administrator in the Warsaw Social Welfare Department. The department provided services to orphans, the poor, and the elderly. Sendler illegally provided clothing, medicine, and money

In 2007, Irena Sendler receives the Order of the Smile in honor of her work with children. For her efforts in rescuing children from the Warsaw Ghetto, Sendler was nominated for the Nobel Peace Prize and made an honorary citizen of Israel.

to Jewish families. She registered them with the agency under fake Christian names and kept them from being visited by social workers by reporting them as having infectious diseases.

When the Warsaw Ghetto was sealed, Sendler became a member of the Council for Aid to Jews and began efforts to rescue Jewish children. Because of her job she had a pass allowing her to enter the ghetto to bring in food and medicine. She found Polish families willing to take in the children. She recruited at least one person at each of the Social Welfare's Department's branches so that she could arrange false documents. She then smuggled the children out of the ghetto. Some were smuggled out in sacks, body bags, and coffins. Others were hidden under loads of goods. Others were taken out through a church with one entrance facing the ghetto and the other facing the "Aryan" side of Warsaw.

On October 20, 1943, Sendler was arrested by the Nazis. Despite being tortured, she refused to reveal the names of those who had helped her, the families that had taken in the children, or the names of the children themselves. She was sentenced to death but the Council for Aid to Jews bribed the authorities to stop the execution. She was freed but lived in hiding from the Gestapo (German secret police). She continued her work for the children. She lived until 2008, when she died at the age of ninety-eight. In all, her efforts saved the lives of 2,500 children.

RELIGION AND EDUCATION IN THE GHETTO

When the ghetto was formed, the Nazis initially banned prayer services. This did not stop people from practicing their religion. Secret prayer groups and yeshivas (religious schools) were established in private homes, and services were carried out in secret. In 1941, the ban was removed and the Great Synagogue, located on Tlomacki Street, was reopened.

When the Nazis enclosed the ghetto, they banned schools within it, except for a limited number of vocational schools run by the Judenrat for the purpose of teaching practical skills needed to perform labor. In 1941, after numerous petitions, the Nazis allowed elementary schools in the ghetto to teach basic skills, presumably for the same reason.

In 1940, members of Jewish educational organizations formed the Consultative Commission and started organizing secret classes in the soup kitchens. The emphasis was on teaching reading and writing, but other subjects, such as Hebrew, Polish, mathematics, history, geography, and science were also taught. Students of college age could take professional or vocational courses administered by the Judenrat. Among these courses were tailoring, mechanical and electrical technical training, lathe operation, locksmithing, chemistry, medicine, and pharmacy. Completing a vocational course could allow people to get a stamp on their identification card exempting them from being taken to a forced labor camp as unskilled labor.

CHAPTER 5

DEATH AND RESISTANCE

By 1941 the process of systematically exterminating the Jews had begun. The Nazis had targeted Poland as the location to perfect their implementation of the "Final Solution," the elimination of Jews. The Nazis established a number of concentration camps in Germany and occupied areas such as Poland. These camps provided a way to concentrate a large group of Jews in one place so that they were readily accessible for whatever activity the authorities deemed desirable.

The first concentration camps were established in 1933 and 1934 as detention and forced labor camps, to contain those whose political views and activities were considered a threat to the Nazi Party. At these camps anyone perceived to be a threat to the Nazis could be detained and made to do hard labor. Eventually, control of concentration camps was taken over by Heinrich Himmler, head of the Nazis' elite security organization, the Schutzstaffel (SS). Under Himmler's direction hundreds of thousands of Jews and other "undesirables," such as Gypsies and communists, were imprisoned in concentration camps.

Some of the most notorious concentration camps were Buchenwald and Dachau in Germany,

Jews in the Warsaw Ghetto were rounded up by German soldiers and taken to concentration camps, where they were killed or made to do forced labor.

and Auschwitz in Upper Silesia on the Polish-German border. The concentration camp to which most of the Jews of the Warsaw Ghetto were deported was Treblinka, 50 miles (80.5 km) northeast of Warsaw. In 1942, the German authorities decided that all Jews were to be transported to these camps. Although some Jews were kept alive to perform labor necessary to the war effort, the majority were killed.

DEATH CAMPS

In the early 1940s, the Nazis began constructing gas chambers at the concentration camps. These were large buildings disguised as hygiene facilities fitted with showers. Arriving Jews were separated into two groups. Those who were deemed suitable to work as forced laborers were sent to the detention camp. The others were sent to hygiene stations that supposedly contained showers. Once inside, they were killed by cyanide gas.

Treblinka was the concentration camp to which the Jews of the Warsaw Ghetto were sent. It was built in 1941 as a forced labor camp. In 1942, a second compound was built, called Treblinka II. Treblinka II housed gas chambers, and its sole purpose was to kill Polish Jews. Two hundred and sixty-five thousand Jews from the Warsaw Ghetto would ultimately be killed at Treblinka, in addition to nearly another five hundred thousand from other areas.

The activities at Treblinka were conducted in great secrecy. The camp was disguised as a way station where people would stop en route to "resettlement" locations, and those being deported from the ghetto were told they were going to be resettled in another location. Upon arrival by train, those deemed suitable for work were separated from the others, mostly women and children. Those not selected for labor were told they were going to a bathhouse and entered the gas chamber. Once they were locked inside, poisonous gas was released. The personal belongings of the Jews were collected, sorted, and sent to Germany for use.

DEPORTATION TO DEATH CAMPS

In the summer of 1942, the Nazis began deporting Jews from the Warsaw Ghetto to the death camp at

Jews who were deported from Hungary are seen here in May 1944 exiting a German boxcar and crowded onto a platform at the Auschwitz concentration camp in Poland.

Treblinka. The first mass deportation consisted of three hundred thousand people. They were loaded on trains at a rate of five thousand to thirteen thousand per day. Initially, Jews being used to work in German factories, hospital workers, Jewish police, and Judenrat officials were exempt. When a second wave of deportations began in January 1943, these special populations became subject to deportation with the other Jews remaining in the ghetto.

DEPORTATION

The following are excerpts from the diary of Abraham Lewin for the period of July–September 1942, published on the Web site of the Holocaust Education & Archive Research Team of HolocaustResearchProject.org. They describe the beginning of the deportations:

> **Wednesday 22 July 1942—The Day Before Tishebov [a Jewish holiday]**
>
> **A day of turmoil, chaos and fear, the news about the expulsion of Jews is spreading like lightning through the town—Jewish Warsaw has suddenly died, the shops are closed, Jews run by, in confusion, terrified.**
>
> **The Jewish streets are an appalling sight—the gloom is indescribable. There are dead bodies at several places—No one is counting them and no names are being given in this terrifying catastrophe.**
>
> **The expulsion is supposed to begin today from the hostels for the homeless and from the prisons. There is also talk of an evacuation of the hospital. Beggar children are being rounded up into wagons.**
>
> **I keep thinking about my aged mother—it would be better to put her to sleep than to hand her over to those murderers. . .**
>
> Friday 24 July 1942
>
> **The turmoil is as it was during the days of the bombardment of Warsaw. Jews are running as if insane, with children and bundles of bedding.**

Mothers and children wander around like lost sheep—where is my child? Weeping. . . Old men and women, boys and girls are being dragged away. . .

[Source: Holocaust Education & Archive Research Team/ HolocaustResearchProject.org. "'Eclipse of the Sun—Universal Blackness' Extracts from the Diary of Abraham Lewin, Warsaw Ghetto—July–September 1942." Retrieved August 26, 2013 (http://www.holocaustresearchproject.org/ghettos/al-diary.html).]

THE WARSAW GHETTO UNDERGROUND

In response to the establishment of the ghetto, underground groups began to form with the aim of resisting the Nazis. The underground consisted of various groups with different political outlooks. They generally met secretly in small groups in soup kitchens. Among the more active groups was the socialist Bund (organization). This group succeeded in getting information regarding the mass executions of Polish Jews to authorities in London in 1942. There were also a number of Zionist organizations in the underground, including the Po'alei Zion, the World Jewish Congress, the Jewish Agencies, and Hehalutz. Zionists sought to have a Jewish state established in the Mideast in the ancient homeland of the Jews. The attempts to exterminate the Jewish population fueled the feeling that such a Jewish state was necessary to protect Jews from extinction in the future.

A GIRL SMUGGLER

Vladka (Fagele ["Little Bird"]) Peltel Meed, who was one of the girl smugglers, recounted her experiences on the U.S. Holocaust Memorial Museum "Personal Histories" Web site. On one occasion she was smuggling 10 pounds (4.5 kg) of dynamite into the ghetto. She had communicated by telephone with her contacts, saying she would be at a certain location and they should meet her. According to Meed, "One of the very easy places which smuggling was going on was on Franciszkanska (Franciscan Street). It was a place where one part of the ghetto, of the wall, was on the side of the Polish side and the other part of the wall was the Jewish side." Many items were smuggled into the ghetto, such as food and clothing, for which the smugglers could get a lot of money. The German patrols couldn't be bribed, but the smugglers bribed the Polish or Jewish police. Meed says,

> **I came there with mine package in greasy paper that it should look like butter, and I paid the foreman . . . and to my luck when I came on top, going on the ladder on top of the wall, suddenly shooting was heard from far away, and they got scared. They snatched the ladder away. And I was sitting on top not being able to go back into hiding. . .And I was with mine package on top of the wall, and the shooting got closer and I was sure that I, this time I am done. I didn't see anybody on the Jewish side and I didn't see anybody on the other side (laughter) and I on top. I didn't know what to do. I was afraid to jump. I was afraid that maybe dynamite can blow up. I didn't know even if it can. . .I didn't know too much about dynamite.**

Luckily for Meed two of her colleagues from the Jewish underground saw her, ran to wall, and got her down.

[Source: "Vladka (Fagele) Petel Meed—Oral History. Transcript." Retrieved September 6, 2013 (http://www.ushmm.org/exhibition/personal-history/media_oi.php?MediaId=2900).

Youth movements were also part of the underground. The members of these groups constituted some of the most energetic and rebellious members of the underground. Prior to the war, youth organizations had primarily been concerned with preparing young people to immigrate to Palestine, teaching them the skills to live communally on a kibbutz (communal farm). After the creation of the Warsaw Ghetto, youth organizations became the center of young people's lives. In these organizations, they provided each other with support and coped with the problems of life in the ghetto. Among their major activities were getting information into and out of the ghetto, and to and from towns around the country. Members of the youth organizations, mostly girls, sneaked out of Warsaw and traveled illegally around the country, gathering information and weapons, and acting as couriers for the Jewish Fighting Organization. Many were caught and killed in the process.

CHAPTER 6

THE GREAT UPRISING

The mass deportations from the ghetto began on July 22, 1942. About 265,000 Jews were sealed in cattle cars and sent by train to the death camp at Treblinka; many died in the overcrowded cars along the way. Approximately another 11,500 were sent to forced labor camps, and about 10,000 were killed by the Germans in the ghetto in the process of carrying out the deportation.

On July 28, the Zydowska Organizacja Bojowa (ZOB, or Jewish Fighting Organization) was formed. Its purpose was to resist the deportations. The ZOB tried to convince the residents of the ghetto to resist the deportations, but initially the organization had little success. Also, the organization itself had two problems. The first was that it was composed of various underground groups. The youth groups wanted to take decisive action and physically resist the Nazis. Some of the other groups feared that violent resistance would lead to the complete destruction of the ghetto. Thus, there was no agreement on what course to take. A second, more practical problem was that the organization lacked weapons.

After the first round of deportations ended, the ZOB reorganized. Now composed of members of the youth organizations, it established a headquarters in a carpentry workshop known as the Ostdeutsche Bauwerkstatte and worked to smuggle in weapons. The leader of the revitalized ZOB was Mordechai Anielewicz.

CONFRONTATION

On January 18, 1943, the Nazis began a second wave of deportations from the ghetto. The Jewish Fighting Organization recruited members to fight, armed them, and built a series of bunkers and barricades. When the Nazis started their 1943 deportations, they were met with

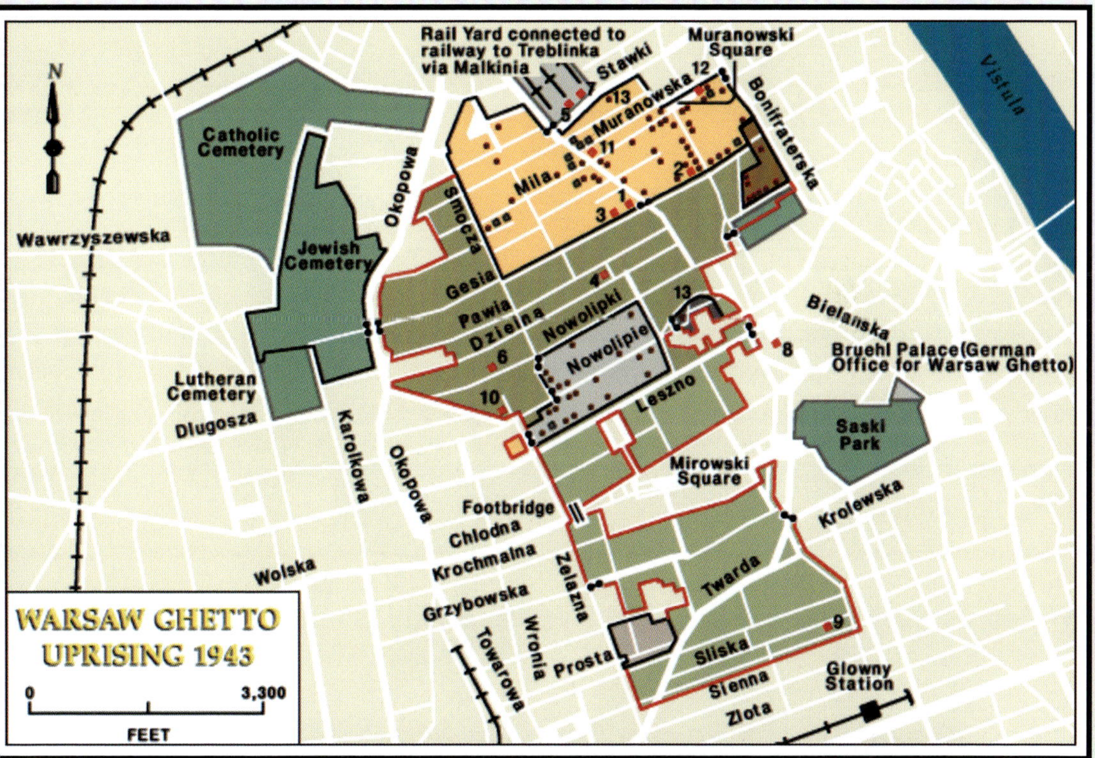

This map shows the ghetto at the time of the uprising and the major points at which activities took place. The railway depot used for deportation is at the top.

armed resistance. As hundreds of Jews were being marched down Mila Street in a long line toward the transport depot, members of the ZOB joined the line. Led by Anielewicz and armed with pistols, they opened fire on the German guards. Other groups of ZOB members joined the line on Mila Street or near the depot and also attacked. A group led by another prominent ZOB leader, Yitzak Zuckerman, led a group of fighters in a residence in Zamenhof Street. The Germans had been forcing their way into houses to extract the occupants. Now they met armed resistance. They were forced to stop going door to door. Many young

German soldiers guard members of the Jewish resistance taken prisoner during the Warsaw Ghetto uprising. About fourteen thousand Jews died during the uprising.

Jewish fighters fell in the battle, and the Germans responded by shooting Jews in the streets. Nonetheless, they were unable to corral most of the Jews slated for deportation. After four days, the Germans were forced to retreat from the ghetto.

The respite was only temporary, however. On April 19, 1943, the Nazis invaded the ghetto with two thousand troops. The resistance was fierce, and the Germans could not defeat the Jewish defenders in direct combat.

German soldiers set fires throughout the Warsaw Ghetto in the aftermath of the uprising. Eventually they destroyed the ghetto completely.

VOICES FROM THE RESISTANCE

The following are comments by members of the resistance who fought in the Warsaw Ghetto Uprising, from the book *Resistance: The Warsaw Ghetto Uprising* by Israel Gutman, published in association with the United States Holocaust Memorial Museum:

> **We started to fortify the posts. The entrance gate was barred by an overturned wagon with its wheels facing upward. We took out cupboards and other pieces of heavy furniture from the apartment and placed them in the entrance way. The windows were shored up with sand-bags. People dispersed to their various posts. [An account of the preparations retold by a fighter in a ZOB squad in the central ghetto]**
>
> **At 4 in the morning, we saw a transport of Nazis moving toward the central ghetto on Nalewki level. Some thousands were marching without end. After that, some tanks go by, armored vehicles, light cannons and hundreds of people of the SS units on bicycles. "They move as if they are going to war," I said to Zippora, a comrade on the post, and I suddenly felt how weak we were. What am I, and what is our strength against this armed and well-equipped army, against tanks and armored cars, and we merely have pistols and, at best, hand grenades? [wrote Simha Ratajzer-Rotem in the fighters' notes]**

In his book *Between Crumbling Walls*, Tuvia Borzykowski, who participated in the first battle, recalls:

At 6 in the morning the siege around the ghetto was already completed. The first units marched on ghetto ground in the direction of Nalewki, approaching the triangle of Nalewki, Gesia, and Franciszkanska. We did not wait for the enemy to be the first to start the slaughter, and from all our posts we showered a hail of bullets and hand-grenades and bombs. Well, our home-made efforts were not so

German soldiers arrest a Jewish resistance fighter. After the uprising, German soldiers went from bunker to bunker under buildings, forcing out the remaining fighters.

VOICES FROM THE RESISTANCE (CONTINUED)

disappointing; they went off as they should and did their work well. . . It was our first confrontation and the bursting bombs proclaimed and told everyone that the uprising has begun. . .

THE FINAL SIEGE

After several days of standoff, the Nazis began to burn down buildings to drive the defenders out. On May 8, the leader of the Jewish Fighting Organization, Mordechai Anielewicz was killed, and their headquarters fell. By late April, the Germans were locating the bunkers that sheltered the resistance by using dogs and sound detectors. They were invariably met with armed resistance if they attempted to enter a bunker. Therefore, after blowing open the entrance to a bunker, they resorted to smoke and poisonous gas grenades to drive the defenders out into the open. On May 8, the Germans attacked the command bunker of the ZOB at Mila 18 using grenades and poison gas. Most of those inside perished, although a few managed to escape. Fighting continued even after the destruction of the command bunker. The Nazis completed destroying the ghetto on May 16. As a final act they blew up the Great Synagogue on Tlomackie Street.

Jürgen Stroop, the commander responsible for destroying the ghetto, issued a report on the action in the Warsaw Ghetto. In this report, referred to as the Stroop Report, he states that 56,065 Jews were caught in the former Jewish quarter, and says, "Of the total of 56,065 Jews caught, about 7,000 were exterminated within the former Ghetto in the course of the large-scale action, and 6,929 by transporting them to T.II [Treblinka II], which means 14,000 Jews were exterminated altogether. Beyond the number of 56,065 Jews an estimated number of 5,000 to 6,000 were killed by explosions or in fires; 631 bunkers were destroyed."

German soldiers search the belongings of Jews rounded up after the Warsaw Ghetto uprising, while frightened Jews huddle, waiting for their turn to be searched.

AFTERMATH OF THE UPRISING

Nearly sixty thousand Jews died during the Warsaw Ghetto Uprising. The Nazis did not succeed in finding every Jew in Warsaw, however, and some continued fighting intermittently until June 1943.

About fifty Jewish fighters were rescued by the People's Guard, a Polish resistance group. These Jewish fighters formed their own resistance group and named it after Anielewicz. Many Jewish resistance fighters joined the regular Polish underground. Others worked in secret to get Jews out of Poland, providing forged documents and assistance. One effect of the Warsaw Ghetto Uprising was to change the image of Jews as people who would accept abuse without fighting back. The events in Poland and similar German-held territories also fueled the belief among many surviving Jews that they would never be safe as long as they were living in a country not their own. This belief was one of the driving forces behind the creation of Israel. The hope was that if Jews had their own country, they would be able to live in safety there.

AFTER THE WAR

On May 8, 1945, Jürgen Stroop surrendered to the U.S. forces in Poland. He attempted to conceal his identity, but the military discovered his reports on the operations in the Warsaw Ghetto. In 1947, he was tried for war crimes at the tribunal at Dachau and sentenced to death by hanging. However, the Americans handed him over to Polish military authorities in Berlin. In 1951, he was taken to Warsaw, where he was tried in court for his actions, found guilty, and again

THE WARSAW GHETTO IN THE MOVIES

A number of movies have been produced that recount events that occurred in Poland and the Warsaw Ghetto. Among them are the following:

The Wall (1982), directed by Robert Markowitz, is a TV movie that is a dramatic re-creation of the Warsaw Ghetto Uprising.

Schindler's List (1993), directed by Stephen Spielberg, tells the true story of German industrialist Oskar Schindler's successful efforts to protect the lives of the Jews who worked in his factories during the war. The film is based on the book *Schindler's List* by Thomas Keneally.

The Island on Bird Street (1997), directed by Soren Kragh-Jacobsen, tells the story of Alex, an eleven-year-old Jewish boy living in a ghetto in German-occupied Poland after his parents are deported. It is based on the semiautobiographical book *The Island on Bird Street* by Uri Orlev.

Edges of the Lord (2001), directed by Yurek Bogayevicz, tells the story of a Jewish boy in Poland who is hidden from the Germans by a Catholic family.

Uprising (2001), directed by Jon Avnet, is a TV movie depicting the events of the Warsaw Ghetto.

The Pianist (2002), directed by Roman Polanski, tells the story of pianist Wladyslaw Szpilman's efforts to survive in the Warsaw Ghetto, where he and his family are forced to move after the invasion of Poland. It is based on Szpilman's autobiographical book, *The Pianist*.

The Courageous Heart of Irena Sendler (2009), directed by John Kent Harrison, is the story of Irena Sendler, the social worker who was part of the Polish underground during World War II.

sentenced to death. On March 6, 1952, he was hanged at Warsaw's Central Prison.

The eastern Warsaw suburb of Praga was liberated in September 1944. In September 1944, the Soviets liberated the main part of Warsaw. Two thousand Jews were found hiding in the remnants of the city. Some Jews returned to Warsaw after the war, with five thousand settling there by the end of 1945 and more joining them after the war. However, anti-Semitism and communist persecution drove most of them out of Poland from the 1940s to the 1960s. Most immigrated to Israel and the United

Jewish resistance fighters who survived the fall of the Warsaw Ghetto pose with survivors of a concentration camp they helped liberate in 1944.

States. The majority of Jews living in Poland today live in Warsaw. Restitution for property taken from Jews by the Nazis remains an issue today.

In 1949, some of the surviving fighters from the Warsaw Ghetto, along with other Jewish partisans and Holocaust survivors, immigrated to Israel and established the Lohamei HaGeta'ot kibbutz. The kibbutz is located in Western Gallilee on the coastal highway between Acre and Nahariya. Its name means "Ghetto Fighters' Kibbutz." The kibbutz engages in agriculture and the production of vegetarian food products. It is home to the Ghetto Fighters' House, which houses a museum and serves as a Holocaust research center.

A memorial to the Jewish uprising in the Warsaw Ghetto was constructed in 1948 in Warsaw and shows a group of resistance fighters armed with guns and Molotov cocktails.

In 1953, the government of Israel passed the law of Yad Vashem. This act created a national memorial to the Holocaust and the resistance. It named the twenty-seventh of Nisan on the Hebrew calendar as a day commemorating the Warsaw Ghetto Uprising (a floating holiday that falls between early April and early May).

Timeline

September 1, 1939 Germany invades Poland, starting World War II.

September 21, 1939 Reinhard Heydrich, head of the German secret police, sends instructions to chiefs of security police in Poland stressing the need to concentrate Jews in urban areas and set up Judenräte.

October 1, 1939 The German army enters Warsaw.

October 7, 1939 The Judenrat is set up in Warsaw with Adam Czerniakow as chairman.

October 26, 1939 The general government is established, and forced labor is decreed for Jews aged fourteen (later twelve) to sixty.

November 1939 The first barbed wire fences are put up at the entrance to streets in the Jewish quarter of Warsaw.

December 1, 1939 It is decreed that all Jews over age twelve must wear an armband with the Jewish star, and all Jewish businesses must be marked.

January 1940 Synagogues are closed, and organized prayer meetings banned.

February 1940 Special ration cards are issued to Jews; they are allowed to purchase goods only in Jewish shops.

October 1940 Construction begins on the walls that will enclose the Warsaw Ghetto.

November 1940 Construction of the walls around the Warsaw Ghetto is completed, and the ghetto sealed. Emmanuel Ringelblum begins the Underground Ghetto Archive.

December 1940 An agency called Transferstelle begins regulating the flow of traffic and goods into and out of the ghetto.

April 1941 Roundups of Jews for the labor camps begin. German companies start setting up factory workshops in the ghetto.

June 1941 The Great Synagogue is opened in Tlomackie Street.

July 1941 The typhus epidemic in the ghetto reaches its peak with about five thousand people per month dying.

September 1941 Efforts to assist the Jews starving in Warsaw reach their peak with 128,000 bowls of soup being served each day.

February 19, 1942 The first groups of Jews are sent to the labor camp at Treblinka. Construction of the death camp Treblinka II begins.

July 1942 The death camp Treblinka II begins operating, and transportation of Jews from the ghetto to the camp begins.

July 28, 1942 The Jewish Fighting Organization is formed.

November 1942 A report by the underground organizations in the Warsaw Ghetto, "The Liquidation of Jewish Warsaw," is written and taken to the West.

December 1942 The Jewish Fighting Organization is reorganized.

January 18, 1943 The second round of deportations begins in the Warsaw Ghetto. The Jewish Fighting Organization responds with armed resistance. After four days, the Germans are forced to stop deportations.

April 19, 1943 The Germans return to the ghetto with two thousand troops. The Jewish Fighting Organization engages them in fierce fighting.

May 8, 1943 The Germans capture the Jewish Fighting Organization headquarters at Mila 18.

May 8–16, 1943 The Germans complete destruction of the Warsaw Ghetto, searching out and destroying remaining bunkers containing Jewish fighters.

May 16, 1943 The Germans blow up the Great Synagogue on Tlomackie Street as a symbol that the Warsaw Ghetto has been destroyed.

Glossary

ABDICATE To give up ruling.

AFFLUENT Financially well-off.

ANTI-SEMITISM Prejudice against Jewish people.

ASSIMILATED Blending in with the native population.

BARRICADE A barrier placed across a street to block it and provide cover for fighters.

BLACK MARKET The illegal buying and selling of goods.

BUNKER An underground chamber fortified for military use.

CHANCELLOR The elected head of the German government in the democracy instituted after World War I.

COLLABORATOR A person who provides help to the enemy during wartime.

CONTAGIOUS Capable of being spread from one person to another.

CORPSE A dead body.

DEATH CAMP A prison camp where prisoners were taken for the sole purpose of killing them.

DECADENT Inferior; leading to decay.

DEPORT To forcibly transport from one place to another.

DERMATOLOGICAL Relating to the skin.

DESTITUTE Without money or financial resources.

DETENTION CAMP A prison camp where prisoners are held for purposes such as performing forced labor. Also called a concentration camp.

EDICT A decree issued by a ruler.

ELIMINATE To get rid of.

EPIDEMIC The spread of a disease to a large number of people.

EXEMPT Not required to do something.

EXTERMINATE Kill.

EXTORT To obtain money from a person by threatening to harm or reveal information about that person.

IMPRESS To force into an activity.

INDOCTRINATE To instill with particular beliefs.

JUDENRAT (pl. Judenräte) A council of Jewish representatives whose purpose was to interface with the German authorities.

KAISER The hereditary emperor of Germany.

KASHA A type of crushed grain, usually buckwheat.

KIBBUTZ A commune-like settlement in which members of a community share work and profit.

KOMMISSAR Commissioner; in the Warsaw Ghetto, the commissioner for the Jewish residential district.

KOSHER Food prepared according to Jewish religious rules and rituals.

LICE Parasitic insects.

MAZOVIA A territory in east-central Poland.

MONEYLENDING Lending money in return for an additional sum, called interest, while the loan is outstanding or when it is repaid.

POGROM An organized attack or massacre, usually aimed at a particular ethnic group.

POPULIST A political movement arising from or appealing to the general population.

PREREQUISITE An activity that must be performed before another activity can take place.

PROFITEERING Making large profits from the sale of scarce or rationed goods.

RAMPANT Raging and widespread.

RANSACK To plunder or aggressively search.

RATIONALE A statement of reasons.

RATION CARD A card or coupon given to people by the government. The coupons allowed the people to purchase a specific amount of a product.

RHETORIC Persuasive language or propaganda.

STAR OF DAVID The six-pointed "Jewish" star, consisting of two interlaced equilateral triangles.

SYNAGOGUE A Jewish house of worship, sometimes called a temple.

SYSTEMATIC In a well-organized, step-by-step manner.

TENEMENT A rundown apartment building.

TUBERCULOSIS A potentially fatal bacterial infection that affects many organs, but most commonly the lungs.

TYPHUS A contagious disease caused by a type of bacteria and spread by lice.

VÖLKISCH MOVEMENT A political movement that glorifies Germany's past cultural and military achievements.

YESHIVA A Jewish religious school.

YOM KIPPUR One of the Jewish high holy days; during Yom Kippur, Jews fast and pray to atone for their sins over the past year.

For More Information

Florida Holocaust Museum
55 Fifth Street South
St. Petersburg, FL 33701
(727) 820-0100
Web site: http://www.flholocaustmuseum.org
This museum displays exhibits and provides educational resources on the Holocaust.

Holocaust Memorial Center
28123 Orchard Lake Road
Farmington Hills, MI 48334
(248) 553-2400
Web site: http://www.holocaustcenter.org
This center maintains a museum and archival research resources, including an oral history collection.

Holocaust Museum Houston
5401 Caroline Street
Houston, TX 77004
(713) 942-8000
Web site: http://www.hmh.org
This museum houses exhibits and offers educational programs for students.

Illinois Holocaust Museum and Education Center
9603 Woods Drive
Skokie, IL 60077
(847) 967-4800

Web site: http://www.ilholocaustmuseum.org
This museum provides interactive exhibits and educates the public about the Holocaust.

Museum of Jewish Heritage
36 Battery Place
New York, NY 10280
(646) 437-4202
Web site: http://www.mjhnyc.org/findex.html
This museum honors those who died in the Holocaust by celebrating their lives, the traditions that they embraced, and their achievements and faith.

Sarah and Chaim Neuberger Holocaust Education Centre
UJA Federation of Greater Toronto
Lipa Green Centre, Sherman Campus
4600 Bathurst Street, 4th Floor
Toronto, ON M2R 3V2
Canada
(416) 631-5689
Web site: http://holocaustcentre.com
This center maintains a museum and memorial and offers educational programs for students.

Simon Wiesenthal Center
1399 South Roxbury Drive
Los Angeles, CA 90035
(310) 553-9036

Web site: http://www.wiesenthal.com
This a global Jewish human rights organization that confronts anti-Semitism, hate, and terrorism and promotes human rights.

U.S. Holocaust Memorial Museum
100 15th Street SW
Washington, DC 20024
(202) 488-0400
Web site: http://www.ushmm.org
This museum displays exhibits and provides publications on the Holocaust.

WEB SITES

Due to the changing nature of Internet links, Rosen Publishing has developed an online list of Web sites related to the subject of this book. This site is updated regularly. Please use this link to access the list:

http://www.rosenlinks.com/DHH/Warsaw

For Further Reading

Altman, Linda Jacobs. *The Warsaw Ghetto Uprising: Striking a Blow Against the Nazis*. Berkeley Heights, NJ: Enslow Publishers, 2011.

Bialowitz, Philip "Fiszel." *A Promise at Sobibor: A Jewish Boy's Story of Revolt and Survival in Nazi-Occupied Poland*. Madison, WI: University of Wisconsin Press, 2010.

Chiga, Krystyna, and Daniel Paisner. *The Girl in the Green Sweater: A Life in Holocaust's Shadow*. New York, NY: St. Martin's, 2012.

Darman, Peter. *The Holocaust and Life Under Nazi Occupation*. New York, NY: Rosen Publishing, 2012.

Deem, James. *Auschwitz: Voices from the Death Camp*. Berkeley Heights, NJ: Enslow Publishers, 2011.

Down, Susan Brophy. *Irena Sendler: Bringing Life to Children of the Holocaust*. New York, NY: Crabtree Press, 2012.

Faber, David. *Because of Romek: A Holocaust Survivor's Story*. New York, NY: Faber, 2005.

Kramer, Clara. *Clara's War: One Girl's Story of Survival*. New York, NY: HarperCollins, 2009.

Laskier, Rutka. *Rutka's Notebook: A Voice from the Holocaust*. New York, NY: Time/Yad Vashem, The Holocaust Martyrs and Remembrance Society, 2008.

Opdyka, Irene. *In My Hands: Memoirs of a Holocaust Rescuer*. New York, NY: Random House, 2004.

Orbuch, Sonia Shainwald, and Fred Rosenbaum. *Here There Are No Sarahs*. Muskegon, MI: RDR Books, 2010.

Pentlin, Susan Lee. *The Diary of Mary Berg: Growing Up in the Warsaw Ghetto*. Oxford, England: Oneworld Publications, 2009.

Pressburger, Chava. *The Diary of Petr Ginz*. New York, NY: Atlantic Monthly Press, 2007.

Rappaport, Doreen. *Beyond Courage: The Untold Story of Jewish Resistance During the Holocaust*. Somerville, MA: Candlewick Press, 2012.

Tomlin, Carolyn. *The Secret Holocaust Diaries: The Untold Story of Nonna Bannister*. Carol Stream, IL: Tyndale House, 2010.

Wiener, Alta. *From a Name to a Number: A Holocaust Survivor's Autobiography*. Bloomington, IN: AuthorHouse, 2007.

Bibliography

Aktion Reinhard Camps/Holocaust Education and Archive Research Team. "Warsaw Ghetto." Retrieved August 18, 2013 (http://www.deathcamps.org/occupation/warsaw%20ghetto.html).

Aktion Reinhard Camps/Holocaust Education and Archive Research Team. "Warsaw Ghetto Uprising." Retrieved August 20, 2013 (http://www.deathcamps.org/occupation/warsaw%20ghetto%20uprising.html).

American-Israeli Cooperative Enterprise. "Irene Sendler." Jewish Virtual Library. Retrieved September 5, 2013 (http://www.jewishvirtuallibrary.org/jsource/biography/irenasendler.html).

American-Israeli Cooperative Enterprise. "Virtual Jewish World: Warsaw, Poland." Jewish Virtual Library. Retrieved August 18, 2013 (http://www.jewishvirtuallibrary.org/jsource/vjw/Warsaw.html#1).

Borzykowski, Tuvia. *Between Tumbling Walls*. 2nd ed. Translated by Mendel Kohansky. Western Galilee, Israel: Ghetto Fighters' House, 1976.

Engelking, Barbara, and Jacek Leociak. *The Warsaw Ghetto: A Guide to the Perished City*. New Haven, CT: Yale University Press, 2009.

Gutman, Israel. *Resistance: The Warsaw Ghetto Uprising*. Boston, MA: U.S. Holocaust Museum/Houghton-Mifflin, 1994.

Holocaust Education & Archive Research Team/HolocaustResearchProject.org. "'Eclipse of the Sun—Universal Blackness' Extracts from the Diary of Abraham Lewin, Warsaw Ghetto—July–September

1942." Retrieved August 26, 2013 (http://www.holocaustresearchproject.org/ghettos/al-diary.html).

Kassow, Samuel D. *Who Will Write Our History? Rediscovering a Hidden Archive from the Warsaw Ghetto*. Bloomington, IN: Indiana University Press, 2009.

London Jewish Cultural Centre. "The Holocaust Explained: Education: The Jewish Experience." Retrieved August 8, 2013 (http://www.theholocaustexplained.org/ks3/life-in-nazi-occupied-europe/impact-on-jewish-communities/education-the-jewish-experience).

Sloan, Jacob, ed. *Notes from the Warsaw Ghetto from the Journal of Emmanuel Ringelbaum*. New York, NY: iBooks, 2006.

U.S. Holocaust Memorial Museum. "Benjamin Meed—Oral History. Transcript." Retrieved September 20, 2013 (http://www.ushmm.org/wlc/en/media_oi.php?ModuleId=10007256&MediaId=1095).

U.S. Holocaust Memorial Museum. "Concentration Camps 1933–1939." *Holocaust Encyclopedia*. Retrieved August 15, 2013 (http://www.ushmm.org/wlc/en/article.php?ModuleId=10005263).

U.S. Holocaust Memorial Museum. "Invasion of Poland." *Holocaust Encyclopedia*. Retrieved August 15, 2013 (http://www.ushmm.org/wlc/en/article.php?ModuleId=10005070).

U.S. Holocaust Memorial Museum. "Personal Histories: Vladka (Fagele) Petel Meed." Retrieved September 6, 2013 (http://www.ushmm.org/exhibition/personal-history/media_oi.php?MediaId=2900).

University of the West of England, Faculty of Humanities, "Languages and Social Sciences, Law Against Overcrowding of German Schools and Higher Institutions of 25 April 1933." Retrieved August 8, 2013 (http://www.ess.uwe.ac.uk/genocide/schools.htm).

WGBH Educational Foundation/PBS. "Ed Herman: My Warsaw Ghetto Memories." *Frontline*, May 14, 2013. Retrieved August 20, 2013 (http://www.pbs.org/wgbh/pages/frontline/biographies/never-forget-to-lie/ed-herman-my-warsaw-ghetto-memories).

WGBH Educational Foundation/PBS. "Treblinka." Retrieved August 16, 2013 (http://www.pbs.org/wgbh/pages/frontline/shtetl/treblinka).

Yad Vashem Shoah Resource Center. "Czerniakow, Adam." Retrieved August 21, 2013 (http://www.yadvashem.org/odot_pdf/Microsoft%20Word%20-%205934.pdf).

Yad Vashem Shoah Resource Center. "Instructions by Heydrich on Policy and Operations Concerning Jews in the Occupied Territories, September 21, 1939." Retrieved August 20, 2013 (http://www.yadvashem.org/odot_pdf/Microsoft%20Word%20-%201984.pdf).

Yad Vashem Shoah Resource Center. "Jewish Fighting Organization, Warsaw." Retrieved August 22, 2013 (http://www.yadvashem.org/odot_pdf/Microsoft%20Word%20-%206370.pdf).

Index

ABOUT THE AUTHOR

Jeri Freedman has a B.A. from Harvard University. She worked for a number of years in the education department of the Anti-Defamation League in programs providing information on the Holocaust to history teachers. She is the author of numerous nonfiction books for students, including *Privacy vs. Security* and *America Debates: Civil Liberties and Terrorism*.

PHOTO CREDITS

Cover (top), pp. 36, 38, 45 Galerie Bilderwelt/Hulton Archive/Getty Images; cover (center) © iStockphoto.com/Steve Christensen; cover (bottom left), p. 55 Sovfoto/Universal Images Group/Getty Images; cover (bottom right), p. 59 Keystone/Hulton Archive/Getty Images; pp. 4–5, 32 Hugo Jaeger/Time & Life Pictures/Getty Images; pp. 8, 29, 40 Imagno/Hulton Archives/Getty Images; p. 12 Central Press/Hulton Archive/Getty Images; p. 13 dpa/picture-alliance/AP Images; pp. 15, 18 Private Collection; p. 17 © AP Images; pp. 21, 53 United States Holocaust Memorial Museum; pp. 22, 47 Hulton Archive/Getty Images; p. 24 Mondadori/Getty Images; p. 27 Fox Photos/Hulton Archive/Getty Images; p. 41 Laski Diffusion-Wojtek Laski/Getty Images; p. 54 Universal Images Group/Getty Images; p. 57 AFP/Getty Images; p. 62 Keystone-France/Gamma-Keystone/Getty Images; p. 63 Tomasz Bidermann/Shutterstock.com; cover and interior page background elements optimarc/Shutterstock.com (gray textures), Gallup Pix/Photodisc/Thinkstock (pillars), Gubin Yury/Shutterstock.com (barbed wire).

Designer: Brian Garvey; Editor: Kathy Kuhtz Campbell; Photo Researcher: Marty Levick